Table of Content

This book provides a comprehensive overview of cybersecurity best practices and their avoidance. It addresses a variety of issues, including establishing a solid security foundation, protecting your online identity, and securing your small business. By adhering to the advice and suggestions in this book, readers can enhance their cybersecurity practices and safeguard themselves and their digital assets from the growing menace of cybercrime.

Chapter 1: Introduction to Cybersecurity: Understanding the Risks and Threats

Cybersecurity is more crucial than ever in the digital age. As our reliance on technology for work, communication, and daily life increases, so does our susceptibility to cyber threats like hacking, identity theft, and data breaches. Cybercrime can have devastating consequences for both individuals and enterprises, including financial loss, reputational harm, and legal repercussions.

This chapter will introduce the subject of cybersecurity and provide an overview of the risks and hazards faced by individuals and organizations. We will discuss the most common forms of cyber-attacks, such as malware, phishing, and social engineering, and provide examples of their impact in the real world. In addition, we will examine the significance of cybersecurity awareness and education, as well as the role of individuals, businesses, and governments in creating a safer and more secure digital world. By the end of this chapter, readers will have a firm grasp on the significance of cybersecurity and the need to take preventative measures to safeguard themselves and their digital assets.

• *The significance of cybersecurity in the current era*

The rapid development of technology has altered how we work, reside, and communicate. As a result of our increased reliance on digital systems for everything from banking to healthcare, our personal and professional lives have become more susceptible to cyberattacks. Cybersecurity has become an essential component of modern life, as we must safeguard our digital assets from hackers, viruses, and other forms of cybercrime.

The sheer volume of data that is now stored digitally is one of the primary reasons why cybersecurity is so essential in the modern climate
. There is a substantial risk of sensitive data straying into the wrong hands due to the abundance of information available online. Personal information, including bank account information, social security numbers, and medical records, is a desirable target for cybercriminals. This information, if compromised, can result in identity theft, financial fraud, and other grave consequences.

Cyber attacks pose a threat to businesses, as hackers frequently target sensitive data such as consumer information, intellectual property, and financial data. A successful cyberattack can cause significant financial and reputational harm, and businesses face legal repercussions if they fail to adequately secure their customers' data.

The increasing prevalence of cyberattacks highlights the significance of cybersecurity. Cybercrime will cause more than $10 trillion in damages by 2025, up from $3 trillion in 2015, according to a report by Cybersecurity Ventures. The report also indicates that cyberattacks are increasing in frequency, with an average of one occurring every 39 seconds.

In addition, the sophistication of cyberattacks is increasing, making them harder to detect and prevent. Traditional security measures are circumvented by hackers employing sophisticated techniques such as social engineering, artificial intelligence, and machine learning. Therefore, individuals and organizations must keep abreast of emerging trends and technologies in order to avoid potential hazards.

The increasing reliance on the Internet of Things (IoT) and connected devices is another reason why cybersecurity is so crucial in the modern world. As more and more devices become internet-connected, the potential attack surface increases exponentially. Any internet-connected device, from smart residences to industrial control systems, is a potential target for hackers.

Lastly, the COVID-19 pandemic has emphasized the significance of cybersecurity in the contemporary world. Businesses have had to adapt to a new method of working as the number of remote workers has grown. This has led to an increase in cyberattacks, with hackers exploiting the vulnerabilities remote working environments present.

Cybersecurity is crucial in the modern world in order to safeguard our digital assets from cyber threats. The prevalence of cyberattacks, the increasing sophistication of hackers, the reliance on IoT and connected devices, and the impact of the COVID-19 pandemic have all highlighted the significance of cybersecurity. Individuals and organizations must take a proactive approach to cybersecurity, keeping abreast of emerging trends and technologies and instituting best practices to guard against potential threats. By adopting these measures, we can make the digital world safer and more secure.

• *A summary of cybersecurity threats and hazards*

Cybersecurity hazards and risks are ever-present in the digital age of today. As our reliance on technology increases, so does our susceptibility to cyberattacks. This article will provide an overview of the most prevalent cybersecurity risks and hazards, as well as their potential effects on individuals and businesses.

Malware is one of the most prevalent cyberthreats. Malware is software designed to cause damage to or obtain unauthorized access to a computer system. Malware consists of viruses, worms, Trojan horses, and ransomware. Malware can cause a variety of problems, including slowing down or crashing systems, stealing sensitive data, and shutting users out of their own devices.

Phishing is another prevalent cyberthreat. Typically, phishing assaults involve the sending of fraudulent emails that appear to originate from a legitimate source, such as a bank or business. The objective of phishing attacks is to obtain sensitive information from the recipient, such as logon credentials or credit card information. Phishing attacks can be complex, with assailants employing social engineering techniques to create convincing fake emails and websites.

Social engineering assaults are a type of cyberattack that manipulates individuals into divulging sensitive information or performing specific actions. These attacks can take a variety of forms, such as impersonating a trusted individual or authority or employing psychological techniques to instill a sense of urgency or dread. As they rely on human psychology rather than technical vulnerabilities, social engineering attacks can be challenging to detect and prevent.

Unsecured Wi-Fi networks represent an additional security risk. Public Wi-Fi networks are readily exploitable, allowing hackers to intercept data sent between devices and the internet. This can include sensitive data like logon credentials or financial information. When using public Wi-Fi networks, users should always exercise caution and avoid transmitting sensitive data over unsecured connections.

Finally, organizations must be aware of the cybersecurity risk posed by insider threats. Insider threats can originate from employees, contractors, or anyone else with access to sensitive information or systems. Insider threats can be intentional, like an employee stealing data for personal benefit, or unintentional, like an employee sharing sensitive information by accident.

Cybersecurity hazards and threats are a major concern in the digital age of today. Malware, phishing, social engineering attacks, unsecured Wi-Fi networks, and insider threats are a few categories of cyber-attacks that individuals and organizations should be aware of. Individuals and organizations must take a proactive approach to cybersecurity to secure themselves, which includes implementing security best practices, keeping abreast of emerging threats, and utilizing dependable cybersecurity tools and services. Through vigilance and preparedness, we can contribute to the creation of a safer and more secure digital world.

• The influence of cyber threats on individuals, organizations, and governments

Cyber threats have become a major concern for individuals, companies, and governments. Cyberattacks can result in a variety of consequences, including financial losses, reputational injury, and even physical harm. The impact of cyber threats on individuals, enterprises, and governments will be examined in this article.

Cyber threats can result in financial losses, identity theft, and privacy violations for individuals. Cybercriminals can pilfer sensitive information such as credit card details, social security numbers, and login credentials, which can be used for identity theft or fraud. This can result in substantial financial losses and credit score injury. In addition, cyberattacks can compromise personal privacy by intercepting private communications or gaining access to sensitive images and videos.

Cyber threats can result in substantial financial losses, reputational harm, and legal liabilities for businesses. Cyberattacks can impede business operations, resulting in costly disruptions and decreased productivity. Moreover, data intrusions can lead to the loss of sensitive information, such as customer data, trade secrets, and financial data. This can lead to reputational harm, consumer distrust, and legal liability. Regulatory penalties and fines may also be imposed on businesses for failing to adequately safeguard sensitive information.

Cyber threats can have significant national security implications for governments. Cyberattacks can be employed to steal sensitive government data, disrupt vital infrastructure, and even cause physical damage. For instance, a cyberattack on a power grid could cause extensive blackouts and economic damage. Cyberattacks can also be used to acquire military secrets or undermine national security operations. Consequently, governments must take a proactive approach to cybersecurity, including the investment in sophisticated security technologies and the development of robust cybersecurity policies and procedures.

Cyber threats can have significant and far-reaching effects on individuals, enterprises, and governments as a whole. Cyberattacks can also result in reputational injury, legal liabilities, and even physical harm. Individuals, businesses, and governments must take a proactive approach to cybersecurity, instituting security best practices, keeping abreast of new threats, and utilizing dependable cybersecurity tools and services. By doing so, we can mitigate the risks associated with cyber threats and create a safer and more secure digital environment.

• *The significance of cybersecurity education and awareness*

The importance of cybersecurity awareness and education has grown as the threat landscape has evolved. Individuals and organizations must comprehend the risks and take proactive measures to protect themselves from cyber threats, which are evolving at an alarming rate. We will discuss the significance of cybersecurity education and awareness.

First and foremost, cybersecurity education and awareness can assist individuals and organizations in comprehending the various cyber threats they face. From phishing and malware attacks to ransomware and advanced persistent threats, cyber threats can range in sophistication. Individuals and organizations can protect themselves from these threats by using strong passwords, keeping software up-to-date, and avoiding suspicious emails and websites, among other measures.

Cybersecurity education and awareness can also assist individuals and organizations in comprehending the significance of implementing best practices to defend against cyber threats. For example, individuals can be taught to use unique and complex passwords, avoid public Wi-Fi networks, and enable two-factor authentication. Organizations can implement policies such as routine data backups, routine security audits, and employee education on how to recognize and avoid phishing schemes. Individuals and organizations can significantly reduce their vulnerability to cyber-attacks by implementing these best practices.

Keeping up-to-date with the most recent threats and trends is a crucial element of cybersecurity awareness and education. Constantly evolving cyberthreats necessitate that you remain informed of emerging threats and new attack techniques. Individuals and organizations can take proactive measures to safeguard themselves, such as installing software patches and updating security settings, if they maintain a state of currency.

Cybersecurity education and cognizance can also assist individuals and organizations in comprehending the potential repercussions of a cyberattack. This may include financial losses, identity theft, and loss of personal data for individuals. Cyberattacks can have even more severe consequences for businesses, including reputational harm, loss of consumer trust, and legal liabilities. Individuals and organizations can protect themselves and mitigate the effects of a cyber-attack by comprehending the potential consequences.

Lastly, cybersecurity awareness and education can contribute to the establishment of a cybersecurity culture within organizations. Organizations can encourage employees to be more vigilant and proactive in safeguarding themselves and the organization by promoting cybersecurity awareness and education. This may involve training programs, routine security audits, and the encouragement of employees to report suspicious activity. By fostering a cybersecurity culture, organizations can significantly reduce their vulnerability to cyberattacks.

In today's digital era, cybersecurity awareness and education are essential. Individuals and organizations can significantly reduce their risk of falling victim to cyber-attacks by understanding the various cyber threats, implementing best practices, remaining current with emerging threats, and fostering a cybersecurity culture. Individuals and organizations must prioritize cybersecurity awareness and education as a vital component of their overall security strategy and treat cybersecurity seriously. Thus, we can contribute to a safer and more secure digital world.

Chapter 2: Developing a Solid Security Foundation: Best Practices for Safeguarding Your Devices

• Realizing the significance of a solid security foundation

To defend ourselves and our devices against these dangers, it is necessary to establish a solid security foundation. We will examine some best practices for safeguarding your devices and private data.

Utilizing robust passwords is the first step in establishing a solid security base. Passwords are the primary means of protecting your devices and accounts, and hackers can readily decipher weak passwords. Therefore, it is imperative to employ complex and unique passwords for each of your devices and accounts. Passwords must be at least eight characters long and contain a mix of uppercase and lowercase letters, numbers, and special characters.

The second stage is to regularly update your software. Frequently, software updates include security upgrades that address software vulnerabilities. Therefore, it is essential to regularly update the software on your devices, including operating systems and applications. Most devices have the option to autonomously download and install updates, ensuring that they are always protected against the most recent threats.

Utilizing antivirus software is another crucial stage in establishing a solid security foundation. Antivirus software can detect and eliminate malware, thereby protecting your devices from cyber threats. Utilizing trustworthy antivirus software and keeping it up-to-date with the latest infection definitions is essential.

In addition to antivirus software, a firewall should also be utilized. Firewalls are designed to prevent unauthorized access to your devices and can prevent malware infections. The majority of devices have firewalls that can be enabled or disabled via the device settings.

Next, it is crucial to exercise caution when using the Internet and opening email attachments. Common cyber threats include phishing attacks, in which cybercriminals attempt to deceive users into divulging sensitive information. Clicking on suspicious links or downloading attachments from unknown sources should be avoided. In addition, it is essential to exercise caution when entering sensitive information, such as credit card numbers or passwords, on websites and to ensure that the site is secure before entering such data.

Using a virtual private network (VPN) is another best practice for securing your devices. A VPN encrypts your internet traffic, making it harder for cybercriminals to intercept and capture your information. VPNs are particularly useful when utilizing public Wi-Fi networks, which are frequently insecure and vulnerable to hacking.

Finally, it is essential to regularly back up your data. By backing up your data, you can defend it from data loss caused by malware, hardware failure, and other catastrophes. It is essential to utilize a secure backup method, such as an external hard drive or cloud storage, and to ensure that the backup is conducted on a consistent basis.

Developing a solid security foundation is crucial for defending your devices against cyber threats. By using strong passwords, keeping software up-to-date, utilizing antivirus software and firewalls, being cautious when browsing the internet and opening emails, utilizing a VPN, and routinely backing up your data, you can reduce your risk of falling victim to cyberattacks significantly. Prioritizing device security and implementing these best practices as a crucial component of your overall security strategy is essential. Thus, we can contribute to a safer and more secure digital world.

• *Using password managers and creating strong credentials*

The creation of robust passwords and the use of password managers have become indispensable for defending personal and sensitive data against cyberattacks. Cybercriminals use various methods, including brute force attacks and social engineering, to access user accounts and pilfer sensitive data. Weak or re-used passwords are readily cracked or guessed, leaving users susceptible to cyberattacks. Strong passwords and password managers come into play at this point.

The first step in securing digital accounts is to create robust passwords. A strong password should be challenging to guess and complex. It must be at least 12 characters long, contain a mix of uppercase and lowercase letters, numbers, and symbols, and exclude readily guessed information such as personal details, common words, or sequential characters. Strong passwords can be difficult to remember, but they offer crucial protection against cyberattacks.

Nevertheless, remembering multiple strong passwords for multiple accounts can be difficult. Here, password managers enter into play. A password manager is a piece of software that stores and manages credentials for multiple accounts. Typically, password managers require users to establish a master password that is used to encrypt and secure all other passwords stored in the manager. Users need only remember the master password in order to access their other credentials.

Password managers offer several advantages over remembering passwords manually. Users can create unique, sophisticated passwords for each account without having to remember them all. This significantly reduces the risk of password reuse and makes it harder for cybercriminals to access multiple accounts if a single password is compromised. Moreover, password managers can automatically generate strong and complex passwords, eliminating the need for users to generate their own strong passwords.

Two-factor authentication provides an extra layer of security by requiring users to provide a second form of identification, such as a fingerprint or SMS code, prior to accessing their credentials. In addition, some password managers feature password auditing, which analyzes the strength and complexity of stored passwords and notifies users of the need to change weak or reused passwords.

There are some potential hazards associated with the use of password managers, despite their benefits. If the master password is compromised, all passwords stored in the password manager are vulnerable. Using a robust and unique master password and enabling two-factor authentication significantly mitigates this risk. In addition, it is essential to select a reputable password manager that employs robust encryption and security protocols to safeguard stored credentials.

The creation of robust passwords and the use of password managers are crucial measures for protecting personal and sensitive data from cyberattacks. Strong passwords must be complex and difficult to predict, whereas password managers provide the convenience of securely storing and managing multiple strong passwords. To ensure maximal security, it is essential to use a reputable password manager and a strong, unique master password. By implementing these best practices, individuals, businesses, and governments can reduce their vulnerability to cyber-attacks and safeguard their sensitive data.

• *Guarding your devices against physical and online dangers*

We are now more reliant on our devices than ever before as a result of technological progress. We rely on these devices, from smartphones to laptops, for communication, work, and entertainment. However, as the use of devices has increased, so has the risk of physical and online attacks. Protecting our devices from these hazards is essential for preserving our privacy and safety.

Theft, damage, or unauthorized access are examples of physical dangers to devices. To protect against tangible threats, it is essential to maintain the physical security of devices. This includes locking devices when they are not in use, not leaving them unattended in public locations, and utilizing anti-theft features such as Find My Device or tracking apps. In addition, it is essential to store devices in a case or cover to prevent damage from drops or accidents.

Malware, viruses, and phishing attacks are among the online hazards to devices. Through malicious websites or email attachments, malware can be downloaded onto devices and used to steal personal information or obtain unauthorized access to devices. Viruses can cause damage to devices and propagate through infected software or files. Phishing attacks consist of deceiving users into divulging sensitive information, such as logon credentials, via bogus websites or emails.

Several recommended practices are required to defend against online threats. First, ensure that all devices have the most recent security patches and software updates installed. These updates frequently include security patches that address known software vulnerabilities and deficiencies. Additionally, it is essential to only obtain software and applications from trustworthy sources, such as official app stores or verified websites.

Antivirus software is another best practice for protecting against online hazards. Antivirus software can detect and eliminate malware and viruses from a device, as well as provide continuous protection against new threats. There are a number of trustworthy antivirus software options available for desktop and mobile devices.

Lastly, protecting yourself from online predators requires practicing good internet hygiene. This may involve averting suspicious links and emails, using strong and unique passwords, and enabling two-factor authentication whenever possible.

In addition to safeguarding against physical and online threats, it is essential to routinely back up device data. Important files and documents will not be lost in the event of a device failure, larceny, or damage if they are backed up. Regular backups should be performed on cloud-based services or external hard drives to ensure the security of the most recent data.

To ensure our privacy and safety, it is essential to protect our devices from physical and online hazards. Theft or unauthorized access can be prevented by employing physical security measures, such as securing devices and anti-theft features. Malware, viruses, and phishing attacks can be defended against by implementing online security measures such as keeping devices updated, utilizing antivirus software, and exercising good internet hygiene. Lastly, routinely backing up device data can prevent the loss of vital data in the event of device failure or damage. Individuals, enterprises, and governments can protect their devices from physical and online threats by implementing these best practices.

• *Maintaining up-to-date software and operating systems*

Software and operating system updates are essential for preserving the security and functionality of any device. Sadly, many users disregard this aspect of device management, leaving themselves vulnerable to a variety of security and functionality issues.

There are a number of factors why it is essential to maintain software updates. The threat of security vulnerabilities is among the most prevalent concerns. Software companies release patches and updates to resolve newly discovered vulnerabilities and threats. Users who do not apply these updates leave themselves vulnerable to security breaches and data theft.

In addition to security concerns, outmoded software can result in performance issues and a reduction in functionality. Software and operating system updates frequently include new features, enhanced performance, problem fixes, and other enhancements. Users who do not update their software lose out on these benefits and may encounter compatibility and stability issues.

Video games provide an entertaining illustration of the significance of maintaining current software. Numerous video games are released with bugs and glitches that adversely affect the gameplay and user experience as a whole. To address these issues, game developers release bug-fixing and performance-enhancing patches and updates. However, players may continue to encounter these issues if they do not download and install these updates.

In the popular game "Minecraft," for instance, a bug was discovered that caused the game to crash when players attempted to access specific game world areas. The developer of the game released a patch that addressed this issue, as well as a number of other problem fixes and enhancements. Those who did not install the patch, however, continued to experience failures and other issues.

Similarly, a bug was discovered in "World of Warcraft" that caused users to be disconnected from the server when they attempted to log in. The developer of the game released a patch that addressed this issue, along with several other issues and performance enhancements. Those who did not implement this patch, however, were unable to log into the game.

Even in the context of video games, these examples demonstrate the significance of maintaining current software. By installing patches and updates, players were able to enjoy a more seamless and functional gaming experience, free of the bugs and glitches that afflicted earlier game versions.

Other forms of software, including productivity software, operating systems, and security software, adhere to the same principles. By maintaining these programs up-to-date, users can protect themselves from security threats, enjoy enhanced functionality and performance, and avoid compatibility and stability issues.

Numerous software applications and operating systems include automatic update functions that make it simple for users to remain current. These features can be configured to automatically obtain and install updates without requiring user intervention. Most programs and operating systems include a "check for updates" feature that allows users who prefer to manually manage their updates to manually download and install updates.

It is essential to keep software and operating systems up-to-date for the security and functionality of any device. Whether you're a video game enthusiast or a business professional, remaining current is of paramount importance. By installing updates and patches, users can protect themselves from security flaws, enhance functionality and performance, and prevent compatibility and stability issues. So, the next time you are prompted to update your software, keep in mind the significance of remaining current and take the time to maintain your device.

• *Understanding the significance of encryption for data protection*

Encryption is a crucial security measure that helps to prevent unauthorized access to sensitive data. It functions by converting plaintext data into a coded format, rendering it unreadable and unusable to anyone without the decryption key. Encryption is essential for preserving personal and sensitive data, such as financial information, login credentials, and other sensitive data.

Encryption is becoming increasingly essential in the digital age, as our reliance on technology to store and transmit data increases. With the rise of cybercrime and hacking, encryption has become an indispensable instrument for securing sensitive data against prying eyes. In this article, we will discuss the significance of encryption and why it is essential for data security.

Encryption is utilized in numerous methods to safeguard data, including data at rest and data in transit. Data at repose refers to information that is stored on an electronic device, such as a computer or mobile phone. In contrast, data in transit refers to information that is being transmitted between devices, such as emails, instant messages, and other online communications.

SSL/TLS encryption, used to secure online communications between websites and users, is one of the most widespread forms of encryption in use today. SSL/TLS encryption functions by establishing a secure connection between the user's device and the website, ensuring that any data transmitted between them is encrypted and cannot be intercepted by hackers or other unauthorized parties.

File-level encryption is a common form of encryption used to secure sensitive files and documents on a device. This type of encryption is particularly useful for preventing unauthorized access to sensitive data such as financial records and legal documents. Combining file-level encryption with other security measures, such as robust passwords and two-factor authentication, provides an extra layer of protection.

Encryption is also necessary for safeguarding mobile devices such as smartphones and tablets, which are especially susceptible to theft and loss. By encrypting data on these devices, users can ensure that their personal data, including contacts, messages, and photographs, cannot be accessed by unauthorized parties.

To illustrate the significance of encryption, let's consider a humorous example. Consider that you are conveying a secret message to your closest friend. You compose the message on a piece of paper and give it to your friend while ensuring that no one else can read it. Therefore, you construct a code that only you and your friend know, such as replacing each letter in the message with the letter that follows it by three positions. The message appears to be a random jumble of letters to everyone else, but to you and your friend, it makes perfect sense. Creating a code that only those who have the decryption key can decipher is essentially how encryption works.

Encryption is an indispensable instrument for safeguarding personal and sensitive data in the digital age. Whether you are using the internet, storing data on a device, or transmitting sensitive data between devices, encryption provides an essential layer of protection against cyber threats and criminals. By grasping the significance of encryption and implementing it in your own life, you can help ensure the safety and security of your data.

Chapter 3: Safe Browsing Techniques: How to Avoid Online Scams and Malware

• *Knowledge of the most prevalent forms of online fraud and malware*

Understanding the most prevalent types of online schemes and malware is essential for defending against cyber threats. As technology advances, so do cybercriminals' methods. They are continually developing new methods to exploit vulnerabilities and deceive individuals into falling for their schemes. This section will discuss some of the most prevalent online schemes and malicious software that you should be aware of.

Phishing schemes are a common form of online fraud in which cybercriminals send emails or messages that appear to originate from reputable sources, such as banks, social media platforms, or online retailers. Typically, these emails or messages contain links that lead to counterfeit websites that appear identical to the originals. These fraudulent websites will then request confidential information, such as login credentials, credit card information, and social security numbers. This information can be used by cybercriminals to steal your identity or perpetrate financial fraud.

Always double-check the sender's email address and verify the legitimacy of any links before clicking on them to avoid falling victim to phishing schemes. Banks and other financial institutions will never request sensitive information via email or text message, so be wary of any such messages. Also, maintain your software and operating systems up-to-date to prevent cybercriminals from exploiting known vulnerabilities.

The tech support scam is another form of online scam. In this scam, cybercriminals will call you or display a pop-up message professing to be from a reputable technology company, such as Apple or Microsoft. They will notify you that your computer is infected with a virus or other issue and offer to fix it for a charge. Once you grant an attacker remote access to your computer, they can install malware and pilfer sensitive data.

Verify the legitimacy of the individual or company contacting you to avoid falling victim to tech support scams. Do not grant remote access to your computer unless you initiated the assistance request. Microsoft and Apple will never contact you directly to inform you of a computer problem, so be wary of unsolicited calls and pop-up messages purporting to be from these companies.

Malware refers to any software that is intended to cause damage to your computer or take your data. It can take the form of infections, spyware, and ransomware, among others. Ransomware is a particularly dangerous form of malware that encrypts your files and demands payment in exchange for the decryption key.

Always use reputable antivirus software and keep it updated to defend against malware. Be cautious when downloading files or following links from unverified sources. Avoid opening email attachments from suspicious senders and installing software from unreliable sources. Ensure that your software and operating systems are up-to-date to prevent cybercriminals from exploiting known vulnerabilities.

Understanding the most prevalent types of online schemes and malware is essential for defending against cyber threats. By understanding these threats, you can safeguard yourself and avoid becoming a victim of cybercriminals. Always confirm the legitimacy of emails, text messages, and phone calls requesting personal information. Keep your software and operating systems up-to-date, and employ anti-malware software from a reputable vendor to defend against malware. By adhering to these best practices, you can establish a solid security foundation and guard against cyber threats.

• *Ability to identify fraudulent emails and websites*

Phishing is one of the most prevalent and perilous forms of cyberattacks. The objective of all phishing attacks is to obtain sensitive information from the victim, such as passwords, credit card numbers, and confidential data.

Typically, phishing emails are intended to resemble emails from reputable sources, such as a bank, social media platform, or e-commerce website. Typically, they will contain a call to action, such as opening a link or downloading an attachment, which will direct the recipient to a malicious website or download malware onto their device.

Phishing websites, also known as "spoofed" websites, are intended to take personal information by imitating legitimate websites. These websites frequently imitate the logos, typefaces, and colors of legitimate websites, making it difficult for the average user to distinguish between the two.

Fortunately, there are numerous methods for identifying fraudulent emails and websites in order to avoid falling victim to these attacks. Here are some advice and illustrations:

1. Examine the sender's email address. Phishing emails frequently originate from email addresses that are nearly identical to those of legitimate senders, but with a minor variation. An email from "support@amaz0n.com" rather than "support@amazon.com" should be considered suspicious.

2. Look for misspellings and grammatical errors. Phishing emails frequently contain misspellings and grammatical errors, as they are frequently written by non-native English speakers. For instance, an email that begins "Dear Valued Costumer" rather than "Dear Valued Customer" is likely phishing-related.

3. Check the URL. Phishing websites frequently use URLs that are nearly identical to those of legitimate websites, but with minor variations. For instance, a fraudulent website might use the URL "bankofamerica-login.com" rather than "bankofamerica.com." Always double-check the URL of the website you are visiting to ensure its legitimacy.

4. Be wary of urgent requests: Phishing emails frequently contain urgent requests, such as "your account has been compromised, please log in immediately to fix the issue." Always be wary of urgent requests and verify the email or website's legitimacy before acting.

5. Do not click on suspicious links or download attachments: Phishing emails frequently contain links or attachments that can

lead to a false website or install malware on your device. Do not act on a link or attachment if you are uncertain about its legitimacy.

6. Utilize anti-phishing software: Numerous antivirus programs offer anti-phishing protection, which can assist in blocking fraudulent emails and websites before they can cause damage.

7. Educate yourself: Keep abreast of the most recent phishing techniques and schemes by reading cybersecurity-related news articles and blogs. You will be better equipped to recognize and avoid phishing attempts the more you learn.

Recognizing phishing emails and websites is crucial for preserving your identity and personal information in the digital age. By following the aforementioned tips and examples, you can remain one step ahead of cybercriminals and protect your sensitive data.

• Employing antivirus software to safeguard your devices against malware

Antivirus software is one of the most essential instruments for protecting your devices against malware. Malware is the abbreviation for malicious software, which consists of viruses, spyware, and other hazardous programs that can infect your computer or mobile device. They are designed to detect and eliminate malware from your system and prevent future infections. It operates by scanning your files and programs for suspicious activity and removing or quarantining any hazards it discovers. There are numerous types of antivirus software on the market, spanning from free to paid subscriptions. Examples of prominent antivirus software include Norton, McAfee, Avast, and Kaspersky.

Always ensuring that your antivirus software is up-to-date is one of the most essential considerations when using such software.

Antivirus software must be able to identify and protect against the continually evolving threats posed by malware. The majority of antivirus programs will update themselves automatically, but it is still prudent to check for updates frequently.

Using antivirus software in conjunction with other security measures, such as a firewall and secure passwords, is also essential for its effective use. Antivirus software cannot defend against all types of security threats, so a layered approach to cybersecurity is essential.

Let's examine some entertaining examples of how antivirus software can protect you from malware.

The Trojan steed is one example.

In Greek mythology, the Trojan horse was a massive wooden horse that the Greeks used to deceive the Trojans into allowing them to enter their city. Similarly, a Trojan horse virus is a type of malicious software that appears harmless but actually contains malicious code that can damage your computer or take your personal data.

Antivirus software can recognize and eliminate Trojan horse pathogens before they can cause damage. It accomplishes this by scanning your files and programs for suspicious activity and then removing or quarantining any hazards it discovers.

Example 2: The Creature

A worm is a form of malicious software that spreads from one computer to another without the user's knowledge or permission. This can be accomplished by exploiting software security flaws or by luring users into opening infected email attachments or clicking on malicious links. By blocking suspicious activity and alerting you to potential hazards, antivirus software can protect you from worms. Additionally, it can monitor email attachments and downloads for malware.

Example 3: Malware

Ransomware is a form of malicious software that encrypts your files and demands a ransom in exchange for the decryption key. It can lead to the loss of crucial data and the interruption of operations, which can be extremely detrimental to both individuals and businesses.

Antivirus software can protect you against ransomware by detecting and eliminating threats before they can encrypt your files. It can also assist with data recovery if your system has already been compromised.

Antivirus software is essential for defending your devices against malware. By keeping your software up-to-date and combining it with other security measures, you can remain one step ahead of cybercriminals and keep your personal data safe and secure.

• *The dangers associated with public Wi-Fi and protection measures*

The proliferation of public Wi-Fi has made it simpler for individuals to remain connected and work remotely, but it has also introduced new risks. Public Wi-Fi networks are frequently insecure, making it simple for hackers to intercept and pilfer data transmitted over them. This chapter will discuss the risks associated with public Wi-Fi networks and how to defend yourself from them.

Dangers of Public Wi-Fi

Public Wi-Fi networks are frequently unsecured, indicating that anyone can connect and potentially access the data of other users. Intercepting data transmitted over public Wi-Fi networks is possible through a variety of means, including the use of packet-sniffing software, the creation of phony access points, and man-in-the-middle attacks.

Packet sniffer software enables hackers to intercept and examine network-transmitted data packets. With this software, cybercriminals can easily steal login credentials and other sensitive information. Creating phony access points is a common method employed by hackers to take data. By establishing a fake access point with a similar identity to a legitimate one, hackers can trick users into connecting to their network rather than the legitimate one. Once connected, the intruder is able to intercept and steal all network traffic.

Man-in-the-middle attacks involve intercepting and modifying communication between two parties in order to steal information or propagate malware. A hacker could intercept data transmitted between a user and a website over a public Wi-Fi network, modify the data, and then submit it to the website. The user would be oblivious that his or her information had been intercepted and possibly compromised.

Safeguarding Yourself from Public Wi-Fi Dangers

You can protect yourself from the hazards associated with public Wi-Fi networks by taking several precautions.

1. Use a VPN

Utilizing a virtual private network (VPN) is one of the most effective methods for protecting data when using public Wi-Fi. A virtual private network (VPN) establishes a secure, encrypted tunnel between your device and the internet, preventing anyone on a public Wi-Fi network from intercepting your data. Your data is encrypted before it leaves your device and is only decrypted when it reaches its destination when you use a VPN.

2. Avoid Accessing Private Accounts

When using public Wi-Fi, avoid accessing sensitive accounts such as your bank account or email. If you are required to log in, ensure that the website is encrypted. Check for the lock icon in the address bar and ensure that the web address begins with "https" rather than "http." Websites that use https encryption are more secure and less susceptible to interception.

3. Utilize Dual Authentication

Two-factor authentication increases account security by requiring a second authentication factor in addition to your password. This may be a code sent to your phone or a scan of your biometrics. Even if hackers have your password, two-factor authentication makes it much more difficult for them to access your accounts.

4. Turn Off Wi-Fi When Not in Use

When not actively using Wi-Fi, disable it on your device. This will prevent your device from connecting automatically to public Wi-Fi networks, which could expose your data to cybercriminals.

5. Utilize infection protection software

Antivirus software can aid in defending your device against malware and other hazards. When connecting to a public Wi-Fi network, ensure that your antivirus software is up-to-date and operating.

6. Employ a Firewall

A firewall is a security system that monitors and regulates network traffic, both incoming and outgoing. Utilizing a firewall can assist in preventing unauthorized access to your device and protecting your data from cybercriminals.

Even with a VPN, it is important to exercise caution when using public Wi-Fi. Avoid accessing sensitive information such as banking or medical records, and always ensure that you are connected to the official network (if available) and not a fake network with a similar name.

In addition to these technical precautions, it is essential to develop safe practices when using public Wi-Fi. Avoid logging into sensitive accounts when using public Wi-Fi, and always log out before exiting the browser. If possible, use a mobile data connection for sensitive duties rather than public Wi-Fi.

In conclusion, public Wi-Fi networks can be a convenient way to remain connected on the go, but they also pose serious risks. You can defend yourself from the dangers of public Wi-Fi by adhering to best practices such as using a virtual private network, avoiding sensitive activities, and practicing good habits.

Chapter 4: Social Engineering: Recognizing and Avoiding Manipulative Techniques

• *Understanding the impact of social engineering on cybersecurity*

Social engineering is a technique employed by cybercriminals to manipulate individuals into divulging sensitive information or performing actions that compromise cybersecurity. It utilizes human psychology and emotions to deceive victims into trusting the assailant and divulging sensitive information.

Social engineering attacks can take a variety of forms, including phishing emails, phony tech support calls, and physical manipulation. For instance, a cybercriminal may impersonate a bank representative over the phone and request the victim's logon credentials and other sensitive information. Another common technique is to send an email that appears to be from a legitimate source, such as a bank or an online retailer, and request that the recipient click a link or input their login credentials.

The "CEO scam" or the "business email compromise" (BEC) assault is an example of social engineering. In this type of attack, the assailant poses as a company executive and sends an employee an email requesting a transfer of funds or sensitive information. The email may appear urgent and persuasive, using language that creates a sense of urgency and a sense of pressure to act immediately.

The "tech support scam" is yet another example of social engineering. In this type of scam, the attacker poses as a tech support representative from a reputable company, such as Microsoft or Apple, and contacts the victim, claiming that their computer is malfunctioning. The attacker then persuades the victim to download software that grants them remote access to the victim's computer, enabling them to take sensitive data or install malware.

Social engineering assaults can have devastating effects on both individuals and organizations. Personal information, bank accounts, and identities can all be stolen from victims. A successful social engineering assault against a business can result in the loss of sensitive information, financial loss, and reputational harm.

To protect yourself from social engineering attacks, it is essential to be cautious and suspicious of any requests for sensitive information, especially if they come from an unexpected or unfamiliar source. Never click on links or download attachments from unverified senders, and always verify the legitimacy of the sender's email address. In addition, be wary of unsolicited phone calls and requests for remote computer access.

In conclusion, social engineering is a potent weapon in the armament of cybercriminals, and understanding how it operates is crucial for defending yourself and your organization against cyber threats. You can reduce the likelihood of falling victim to a social engineering attack by remaining vigilant and adhering to best practices, such as authenticating requests for sensitive information and avoiding unsolicited messages or calls.

• *The most prevalent social engineering techniques*

Social engineering is a type of cyberattack in which individuals are coerced into divulging sensitive information or conducting actions that compromise their security. Social engineering attacks are increasing in frequency and can take many forms, such as phishing emails, phone schemes, and pretexting. It is crucial to comprehend the most prevalent types of social engineering attacks and how to recognize and prevent them.

The most prevalent type of social engineering attack is phishing. It involves sending emails that appear to originate from reputable sources, such as banks, online retailers, or social media platforms, in an attempt to deceive the recipient into divulging sensitive information or clicking on a pernicious link. Phishing emails are designed to appear legitimate, with identical logos and branding to the actual company. In addition, they may contain urgent or menacing language, which can induce a sense of panic and cause the recipient to act rashly.

The 2016 hack of John Podesta's email account, who served as the campaign chairperson for Hillary Clinton's 2016 presidential campaign, is one of the most infamous examples of phishing. The attackers sent a phishing email that purported to originate from Google to Podesta's email address. The email requested that Podesta alter his password, and when he clicked the link he was redirected to a fake Google page where he entered his password. This enabled the attackers to access Podesta's emails and other sensitive data, which they then released to the public.

Pretexting is another prevalent type of social engineering attack. An attacker creates a fictitious scenario to obtain access to sensitive data or information. For instance, an attacker may contact a company employee while posing as a coworker or external service provider. Using the pretense of requiring access to a particular system or application, the attacker may then request the employee's login credentials or other sensitive information.

The 2018 cyberattack on Twitter CEO Jack Dorsey's account is an example of a pretexting attack. Using a technique known as SIM swapping, the attackers convinced Dorsey's mobile carrier to relocate his phone number to a new SIM card. Using this phone number, the assailants reset Dorsey's Twitter password and gained access to his account.

Baiting is a type of social engineering attack in which an assailant leaves a physical device or piece of media, such as a USB drive or a CD, in a public location. The device is typically labeled in a manner that suggests it contains sensitive or valuable information, such as "Employee Salaries" or "Confidential Project Data." When an unsuspecting victim picks up the device and inserts it into their computer, they unknowingly install malware onto their system, compromising their security.

In 2016, an assailant in the United States left USB drives in the parking lot of a nuclear power plant as an example of a baiting attack. The drives were labeled "Employee Training," and when an employee inserted one into their computer, malware was installed, granting the intruder access to the facility's computer systems.

To protect against social engineering attacks, it is crucial to be vigilant and suspicious of any requests for sensitive information or actions that appear odd or out of the ordinary. Always verify the identity of the requesting individual or organization, and never divulge personal or sensitive information over the phone or via email. Use robust passwords and two-factor authentication to safeguard your online accounts, and update your security software and operating systems on a regular basis to ensure that they are protected against the most recent threats.

It is crucial to comprehend the most common types of social engineering attacks and how to prevent them, as they are becoming increasingly sophisticated and widespread. By understanding the risks and taking precautions, you can reduce the likelihood of falling victim to these types of attacks and ensure the security of your personal and sensitive data.

• *Advice for recognizing and avoiding cons*

Scammers are becoming increasingly inventive in their schemes to defraud individuals of their hard-earned cash. From false job postings to phishing emails, it can be challenging to recognize scams and avoid falling victim. However, with some fundamental awareness and knowledge, you can avoid the majority of scams.

The first step in avoiding fraud is recognizing the most prevalent varieties. One of the most common types of deception is phishing, which entails sending fraudulent emails or messages that appear to originate from a legitimate source, such as a bank or online retailer. Typically, these emails contain a link to a bogus website that requests sensitive information, such as your login credentials or credit card number. Once the con artist obtains this information, he or she can use it to pilfer your money or your identity.

A common scam is the tech support scam, in which a person poses as a tech support agent and requests remote access to your computer to repair an alleged problem. In reality, they install malware that can steal your confidential data or encrypt your files and demand a ransom in exchange for their release.

There are also a variety of employment schemes that target job seekers, including those that require payment for job applications or ask for personal information in advance. In some instances, these cons are so sophisticated that they entail phony job interviews.

To avoid falling victim to hoaxes, it is crucial to be vigilant and suspicious of any communication or offer that seems too good to be true. Among the guidelines for recognizing and avoiding cons are:

Before clicking on any links or responding to any communications, you should conduct research on the source. Check online for reports of fraud or schemes involving the company or organization. Check their website to see if their communication manner and branding are consistent.

• Never give out personal information, such as your social security number or credit card number, unless you are certain that the request is legitimate. Even then, it is essential to ensure that the communication is secure and coming from a reliable source.

• Check for misspellings and grammatical errors. Numerous schemes originate from non-English speaking nations and frequently contain misspellings and grammatical errors. Be suspicious of any communication containing such errors.

• Do not believe everything you read; con artists frequently use fear tactics and false promises to convince victims to act. Be wary of any communication that attempts to coerce you into taking immediate action or making an immediate payment.

Install and update anti-virus and anti-malware software on your computer and mobile devices on a regular basis. This can assist in detecting and preventing numerous varieties of fraud and malware.

• Rely on your intuition: if something seems off or too good to be true, rely on your intuition and avoid the communication or offer.

Additional suggestions for recognizing and avoiding fraud:

a. Be wary of unsolicited emails and phone calls: con artists frequently pose as representatives of well-known companies or organizations when sending unsolicited emails and making unsolicited phone calls. Be cautious if you receive an unexpected email or phone call from someone professing to represent a company or organization. Avoid providing personal information or acting on any links until you can confirm the request's legitimacy.

b. Check the URL. Scammers frequently construct websites that closely resemble the real thing. However, the website's URL can frequently reveal whether or not it is legitimate. Before entering any personal information or making a purchase, always verify the URL. Check for the lock icon in the address bar and ensure that the URL begins with "https://" as opposed to "http://"

c. Be wary of urgent requests, as con artists frequently use urgency to induce hasty decisions. For instance, they may assert that there is an urgent issue with your account or that you have won a reward but must act quickly to claim it. If someone is pressuring you to act quickly, it is always advisable to take a step back and assess the situation attentively.

d. If something appears to be too wonderful to be true, it most likely is. Scammers frequently use the guarantee of large sums of money or other prizes to persuade individuals to reveal their personal information. If you receive an offer that seems too good to be true, you should trust your intuition and proceed with caution.

e. Two-factor authentication is a security measure that requires users to provide two forms of identification before gaining access to an account. Even if fraudsters obtain your password, this can prevent them from accessing your accounts. Numerous websites and services offer two-factor authentication as an option; therefore, it is advisable to utilize this feature whenever feasible.

f. Ensure that your software is up-to-date: Keeping your software up-to-date is essential to your internet safety. Frequently, software updates include security patches that resolve known vulnerabilities, making it more difficult for cybercriminals to exploit your system. Check for updates to your operating system, web browser, and other software programs on a regular basis.

By following these guidelines and being aware of common schemes, you can avoid the majority of fraudulent actions. It is important to keep in mind that con artists are constantly devising new ways to defraud people, so it is essential to remain informed and up-to-date on the most recent scams and techniques. The greatest defense is frequently awareness and prudence, as well as taking the time to evaluate any requests for personal information or financial transactions thoroughly.

• *Protecting your sensitive information against social engineering*

Social engineering is a tactic employed by cybercriminals to coerce individuals into disclosing sensitive information or performing actions that could compromise their personal data and security. It is a form of psychological manipulation that takes advantage of human nature, trust, and curiosity to obtain unauthorized access to protected systems, steal identities, and engage in fraudulent activities. Social engineering attacks can occur anywhere, including online, over the phone, and in person, and they can take a variety of forms, including phishing emails, pretexting, and enticing.

Social engineering attacks can have severe consequences, including financial loss, identity theft, reputational harm, and legal liability. Therefore, it is essential to safeguard your personal information against social engineering techniques. Here are a few considerations:

Be wary of unsolicited communication: If you receive an email, text message, phone call, or social media message from a person you do not know requesting personal information or imploring you to click on a link or download an attachment, be skeptical. Do not accept the message at face value, and refrain from responding or engaging with the sender before verifying their identity and intent.

If the communication appears to originate from a reputable organization or a well-known individual, but you are uncertain, verify the sender's identity. For instance, if your bank sends you an email requesting you to update your account information, you should not click the link in the email. To validate the legitimacy of the request, visit the bank's website or call their customer service line.

Keep your personal information confidential: Do not share your social security number, bank account information, passwords, or login credentials with anyone, particularly if you do not know them or are uncertain of their identity. Sharing personal information online, such as on social media platforms or public forums, where it could be readily accessed by cybercriminals, should also be avoided.

Strong passwords and multi-factor authentication are essential for protecting your online accounts against social engineering assaults. Utilize complex and unique passwords for each account, and whenever possible, enable multi-factor authentication. Thus, even if a cybercriminal guesses your password or steals it via deception, they will be unable to access your account without your permission.

Ensure that your software and devices are up-to-date: Keeping your software and devices up-to-date is an additional crucial measure for protecting your personal information from social engineering attacks. Frequently, software updates include security patches and issue fixes that address known vulnerabilities that can be exploited by cybercriminals. Consequently, ensure that you routinely install updates and enable automatic updates whenever possible.

Educate yourself and others: The key to preventing social engineering techniques is to educate yourself and others about them. Share your knowledge of the most recent social engineering techniques and trends with your friends, family, and coworkers. You can reduce the risk of falling victim to social engineering attacks and safeguard your personal information and security by being aware and prepared.

A combination of awareness, skepticism, and best practices is necessary to protect your personal information from social engineering. By adhering to these guidelines, you can remain ahead of cybercriminals and protect your digital life. Remember that if something seems too good to be true or too imperative, it is likely an attempt at social engineering. remain vigilant and remain safe!

Chapter 5: Best Practices for Secure Communication

• *The significance of communication security in the digital age*

Today, digital channels such as email, instant messaging, and social media platforms are widely used for communication. With the rise of digital communication, it is essential to consider the safety of the shared information. Cybercriminals and hackers are constantly searching for ways to exploit vulnerabilities in these communication channels in order to steal sensitive data or obtain unauthorized access to systems.

Secure communication is the practice of transmitting information over digital channels in a manner that prevents interception and unauthorized access. This involves employing multiple security measures, such as encryption and two-factor authentication, to ensure that only the intended recipients have access to the transmitted information.

Encryption is one of the most essential aspects of secure communication. Using a cryptographic algorithm, encryption is the process of converting plaintext data into an unintelligible format. This makes it extremely difficult for anyone who intercepts the data without the encryption key to decipher it. There are numerous varieties of encryption algorithms, each with its own advantages and disadvantages. It is essential to choose a method of encryption that is suitable for the type of data being transmitted.

Using Transport Layer Security (TLS) encryption, for example, email communication can be secured. This is a protocol that encrypts emails while they are in transit, making it difficult for anyone to intercept and read their contents. It is important to ensure that TLS encryption is enabled on your account, as many email providers use it automatically when sending and receiving messages.

Two-factor authentication (2FA) is another essential element of secure communication. 2FA increases the security of digital communication by requiring users to provide two forms of identification prior to account access. This could consist of a password and a biometric scan or a password and a security token. By requiring two forms of identification, cybercriminals will have a much more difficult time accessing your account.

Social media platforms are another prevalent means of online communication. However, cybercriminals frequently target these platforms to steal personal information or disseminate malware. To secure yourself on social media, it is essential to be cautious about the information you share and the individuals with whom you share it. Ensure that your account is set to private and that you only take friend requests from individuals you know and trust.

Using a virtual private network (VPN) is another method for securing communication. A virtual private network (VPN) is a service that encrypts internet traffic between your device and the VPN server. This makes it extremely challenging for anyone to intercept your internet traffic and observe your online activity. VPNs are particularly useful when using public Wi-Fi networks, which are frequently insecure and can be exploited by hackers with relative ease.

In addition to these precautions, it is essential to be aware of scams and phishing attacks designed to take your personal information. For instance, you should never click on links in unsolicited emails or provide personal information to untrusted websites. Additionally, you should be cautious when downloading files from the internet, as they may contain malicious software or infections.

In the digital era, secure communication is necessary to protect your personal and sensitive information from hackers and cybercriminals. Encryption, two-factor authentication, virtual private networks (VPNs), and awareness of common scams and phishing assaults are a few ways to ensure secure communication. By taking these precautions, you can safeguard your information in the online world.

• *Introduction to ciphering and secure communication tools*

As we continue to use digital technologies for communication, ensuring that our conversations are secure and protected from prying eyes becomes increasingly essential. Secure communication refers to the methods and techniques used to safeguard the secrecy and integrity of data transmitted over digital channels. This includes voice and video communications as well as email, instant messaging, and social media messages.

Encryption is one of the primary methods used to ensure secure communication. Encryption is the process of encoding data so that only authorized parties can access it. Encryption is the process of transforming plaintext into ciphertext, which can only be decoded with the appropriate decryption key. This ensures that even if the message is intercepted by an unauthorized party, it cannot be read.

There are numerous techniques and algorithms for encrypting digital communications. Among the most prevalent is symmetric encryption, which encrypts and decrypts the message using the same key. A further type of encryption is asymmetric encryption, which employs two distinct keys - one for encryption and the other for decryption.

In addition to encryption, several tools and technologies for secure communication can be used to safeguard digital conversations. One of the most prevalent is the Virtual Private Network (VPN), which establishes a secure, encrypted connection between the user's device and the internet. This prevents hackers and snoops from intercepting a user's Internet traffic.

Secure Sockets Layer (SSL) and Transport Layer Security (TLS) are two secure communication protocols used to secure online transactions and prevent data theft. These protocols ensure that all information transmitted between the user's device and the website is encrypted and cannot be accessed by unauthorized parties.

End-to-end encryption is an additional method used to secure communication. This method encrypts messages on the device of the sender and decrypts them on the device of the recipient. This means that even if the communications are intercepted during transmission, they are unreadable to anyone without the decryption key.

In today's digital era, the importance of secure communication cannot be overstated. With the prevalence of cyberattacks and data intrusions on the rise, it is imperative that we safeguard our digital conversations from prying eyes. We can protect our messages and conversations from unauthorized access and interception by utilizing encryption and other secure communication tools.

The 2013 Edward Snowden disclosures serve as an illustration of the importance of secure communication. Snowden, a former contractor for the National Security Agency (NSA), released classified information about the United States government's surveillance programs to the media. Snowden used encrypted email services and other secure communication tools to safeguard his conversations and prevent the NSA and other agencies from intercepting his communications.

Secure communication can also help protect against corporate espionage and cyberattacks, in addition to safeguarding against government surveillance. By encrypting communications and utilizing secure communication tools, businesses can prevent competitors and hackers from stealing their confidential information and intellectual property.

In the digital age, the significance of secure communication cannot be emphasized. By using encryption and other secure communication tools, we can safeguard our digital conversations and ensure that only authorized parties can read our communications.

• Security tips for email and communications

As more of our communication moves online, ensuring that our messages are secure and protected from inquisitive eyes becomes increasingly important. Utilizing encryption and other secure communication tools is one of the most efficient methods to achieve this goal.

Encryption is the process of encrypting data so that it can only be deciphered by those who have the corresponding key. When you transmit an encrypted message, you and the intended recipient are the only ones who can decipher it. This makes it considerably more challenging for hackers and other malicious actors to intercept and read your communications.

There are numerous tools for secure email and communications, each with its own advantages and disadvantages. These are some of the most prevalent options:

PGP (Pretty Good Privacy): PGP is a free and open-source encryption utility that is widely regarded as one of the most secure available options. It has been used for many years by journalists, activists, and other high-risk users to secure their messages using a combination of symmetric and asymmetric encryption.

Signal is a free, open-source messaging application that is widely regarded as one of the safest options for mobile devices. It protects your communications with end-to-end encryption and supports voice and video calls.

ProtonMail is a secure email service with its headquarters in Switzerland. It protects your communications with end-to-end encryption and supports features such as two-factor authentication and self-destructing messages.

When it comes to secure email and messaging, it is essential to remember the following:

Use robust passwords to protect your accounts from cybercriminals. Ensure that your password is between 8 and 12 characters long and contains a blend of letters, numbers, and special characters.

Two-factor authentication increases the security of your accounts by requiring a code in addition to a password. Numerous secure messaging applications support two-factor authentication; therefore, you should enable this feature whenever possible.

Be wary of emails or messages from unverified senders, as they may be part of a phishing scam. Before clicking on any links or downloading any attachments, always confirm the identity of the sender.

Do not send sensitive information via email. Even with encryption, email is not an entirely secure mode of communication. Avoid transmitting sensitive information via email, such as passwords or financial data. Instead, use a secure messaging application.

Encryption and other secure communication tools can assist in protecting your communications from prying eyes in the digital age. By following these guidelines and utilizing the appropriate tools, you can ensure the security of your online communications.

• *How to safeguard your confidentiality during video conversations*

In the era of remote work and virtual meetings, video calls have become a prevalent method of communication for both individuals and businesses. However, the convenience of video conversations comes with the possibility of privacy breaches. Unsecured video conversations can result in unauthorized access to sensitive data, such as personal information, financial data, and business secrets.

You can safeguard your privacy during video conversations by taking the following steps:

• Select a secure platform for video conferencing: Selecting a secure video conferencing platform is the first step in safeguarding your privacy during video calls. Consider platforms with end-to-end encryption, two-factor authentication, and additional security features.

• Use a virtual background: Some video conferencing platforms allow you to obscure your surroundings with virtual backgrounds. This is especially helpful if you are in a public area or if sensitive information is visible in the background.

• Verify your camera and microphone settings Before initiating a video contact, verify that your camera and microphone settings are properly configured. Cover your built-in camera with tape or a webcam cover when it is not in use to prevent unauthorized access.

• Avoid sharing sensitive information: During video calls, avoid sharing sensitive information such as passwords or financial data. Use secure messaging or email instead to transmit this information.

• Use a secure internet connection: When participating in a video call, ensure that you are using a secure internet connection. Avoid using public Wi-Fi, as it can be compromised readily.

• End the call effectively: When you are finished with the video call, ensure that the call is terminated correctly and that you exit the platform. This will aid in preventing unauthorized call access.

In addition to these measures, it is essential to remain current on the most recent security threats and best practices for video conferencing. By adhering to these guidelines and remaining vigilant, you can safeguard your privacy during video calls and reduce the likelihood of privacy breaches.

Chapter 6: Best Practices for Managing Your Digital Footprint.

• *Knowledge of the dangers of online identity theft*

Identity theft online is a prevalent hazard that many people face today. As more of our lives are conducted online, our personal information becomes increasingly susceptible to theft by cybercriminals. This section will cover the dangers of online identity theft, how it occurs, and what you can do to defend yourself.

Theft of a person's confidential and financial information via the Internet is referred to as online identity theft. This may involve the theft of credit card numbers, social security numbers, email addresses, usernames and passwords, and other sensitive information. Once obtained, this information can be used for identity theft or financial fraud.

There are numerous online methods by which cybercriminals can obtain your personal information. One prevalent method is phishing schemes. These are fraudulent emails or messages that appear to originate from a reliable source, such as your bank or a government agency, but are designed to fool you into divulging your personal information.

Another prevalent method is data breaches. When businesses and organizations have inadequate security measures in place, it is simpler for cybercriminals to breach their systems and steal customer data. This data can then be sold to other cybercriminals on the dark web or used to perpetrate financial fraud.

Identity theft can have devastating effects on victims. Not only can it result in financial losses, but it can also harm your credit score and make obtaining credit in the future more difficult. In addition, it may take a considerable quantity of time and effort to repair the damage to your credit and reputation.

There are several measures you can take to protect yourself from online identity theft. It is essential to exercise caution when sharing personal information online. Only provide your personal information to reputable sources, and be wary of emails or messages requesting such information.

Monitoring your credit reports and bank accounts on a regular basis for any suspicious activity is a further essential step. Report immediately to your bank or credit card company any unauthorized charges or activities.

Additionally, you can safeguard your online accounts. Use strong and unique passwords for each account, and whenever practicable, enable two-factor authentication. This increases the security of your account by requiring a second verification method, such as a code sent to your phone, in order to access it.

Additionally, use public Wi-Fi networks with caution. Insecure public Wi-Fi networks make it simpler for cybercriminals to intercept your data. Use a virtual private network (VPN) to encrypt your data and protect your privacy when using a public Wi-Fi connection.

Online identity theft is a grave hazard with far-reaching ramifications for victims. You can significantly reduce your risk of falling victim to this type of cybercrime, however, by taking the necessary precautions to secure your personal information online. Be wary when sharing personal information online, routinely monitor your accounts, protect your online accounts with robust passwords and two-factor authentication, and utilize a VPN when using public Wi-Fi. By taking these precautions, you can protect your online identity and finances.

• *Security best practices for online accounts*

We rely on online accounts for everything from social media to online finance, as they are a fundamental aspect of modern life. Cyberattacks can compromise our sensitive data, personal information, and financial assets. Consequently, securing our online accounts is necessary to prevent online identity theft.

Best practices for securing your online accounts are as follows:

• Use strong, unique passwords: Using strong, unique passwords for each account is one of the most important measures for securing your online accounts. A robust password should be at least 12 characters long and contain a combination of uppercase and lowercase letters, numbers, and symbols. Also, avoid using prevalent words or phrases and personal information in your password, such as your name or date of birth. Consider utilizing a password manager to generate and securely store complex credentials.

• Enable two-factor authentication Two-factor authentication (2FA) is an additional security measure that requires you to provide two forms of identification, such as a password and a one-time code sent to your phone or email, in order to access your account. Enabling 2FA provides an additional layer of security against cybercriminals who may have acquired your password.

Ensure that all of your software, including your operating system, web browser, and applications, is up-to-date with the latest security upgrades and updates. Cybercriminals frequently exploit software vulnerabilities to gain access to your online accounts and take your personal data.

• Avoid using public Wi-Fi. Public Wi-Fi networks are notoriously insecure, and hackers can intercept your online traffic and take your login credentials with relative ease. Use a virtual private network (VPN) or avoid using public Wi-Fi networks to access your online accounts.

• Be wary of phishing scams: Phishing is one of the most common methods hackers use to take login credentials and other sensitive data. They typically involve an email or message that appears to come from a reliable source, such as your bank or social media platform, and requests that you click on a link or provide personal information. Avoid clicking on suspicious links and providing sensitive information in response to such communications.

• Regularly monitor your accounts: Monitoring your online accounts for suspicious activity on a regular basis is a crucial step in detecting and averting online identity theft. Check your account activity, including login history, transactions, and settings, and promptly notify the account provider of any suspicious activity.

It is essential to secure your online accounts to prevent online identity theft. By adhering to these best practices, you can substantially reduce the risk of cyberattacks and protect your sensitive data and personal information.

• *Managing your social media presence for privacy protection*

The use of social media has become an integral component of our everyday lives. It allows us to connect with friends and family, share our thoughts and experiences with the world, and remain abreast of current events. However, the pervasive use of social media has also generated privacy and security concerns. Cybercriminals can use personal information posted on social media for identity theft, social engineering attacks, and other malicious activities. To safeguard your privacy, it is essential to manage your social media presence.

Here are some suggestions for managing your social media presence and safeguarding your privacy:

1. Review Your Privacy Settings Social media platforms provide a variety of privacy settings that allow you to control who can view your posts, personal information, and activity. Review your privacy settings frequently to ensure that the information you are sharing with others is acceptable. Ensure that only people you trust can view your profile and posts, and avoid sharing sensitive information such as your home address or phone number.

2. Consider Your Posts Carefully: Think before posting anything on social media. Once something has been posted, it can be

difficult to eliminate it entirely. Avoid disclosing information that could be used to identify you, such as your full name, date of birth, and birthplace. Also, be cautious about revealing your location, as doing so can expose your location to potential criminals.

3. Utilize Strong Passwords: Use unique, robust passwords for all of your social media accounts. Avoid reusing passwords across multiple accounts, as this can increase the likelihood of a security breach. Consider enabling two-factor authentication, which provides an additional layer of protection for your accounts.

4. Be Cautious of Scams: Social media is frequently used by cybercriminals to initiate phishing attacks and scams. To steal your confidential information, they may send you a message or a friend request posing as a trusted entity, such as your bank or a government agency. Avoid clicking on links or downloading attachments from unverified sources.

5. examine Your Activity On a regular basis, examine your social media activity to ensure that no suspicious activity has occurred on your account. Verify the legitimacy of all of your posts, comments, and likes. Immediately report any unauthorized activity to the social media platform if you observe it.

6. Limit Third-Party Access: Be wary of the applications and websites to which you grant access to your social media accounts. Some third-party applications may need access to your personal data in order to function properly. However, exercise caution when disclosing sensitive information such as your location or email address.

7. Educate Yourself on Social Media Security: Educate yourself on the threats and best practices associated with social media security. Follow security professionals and organizations that specialize in

online privacy and security to remain abreast of the most recent threats and vulnerabilities.

Managing your social media presence is essential for online privacy protection. By adhering to these best practices, you can minimize the risks associated with social media and maximize the benefits of maintaining connections with others. Keep in mind that your personal information is valuable and that it is your responsibility to safeguard it.

• *Guidelines for safeguarding your personal data online*

As more of our activities move online, it becomes more important to safeguard our personal information. From financial data to sensitive personal information, it is crucial to protect our data from cybercriminals who are continuously searching for exploitable vulnerabilities. Here are some guidelines for safeguarding your personal data online.

1. Software vulnerabilities are one of the most prevalent means by which cybercriminals obtain access to your information. Maintain your operating system, web browser, and all applications with the most recent security upgrades and updates.

2. Use strong passwords: A strong password consists of at least eight characters and a mixture of uppercase and lowercase letters, numerals, and special characters. Avoid using readily guessed passwords such as "123456" or "password." Instead, use a unique, easily-remembered passphrase.

3. Two-factor authentication provides an additional layer of security for your accounts. In two-factor authentication, in addition to your password, you must provide an additional form of identification, such as a code sent to your phone.

4. Be wary of phishing emails: Phishing emails are designed to appear like legitimate emails from reputable sources, but they are actually bogus emails intended to trick you into divulging personal information. Be wary of emails that request your login credentials or financial information, and never download files or click on links from unknown sources.

5. Employ a virtual private network (VPN): A VPN encrypts your internet traffic and conceals your IP address, making it harder for cybercriminals to trace your online activity. When using public Wi-Fi or accessing sensitive information online, use a VPN.

6. Check your privacy settings. Social media sites and other online platforms frequently capture and share a great deal of personally identifiable information about their users. Regularly review your privacy settings to ensure that you are only sharing the information you intend to share.

7. Utilize anti-malware software to defend your computer and mobile devices from viruses, malware, and other online threats. Ensure you have installed and regularly updated anti-malware software.

8. Be cautious when using public Wi-Fi networks, as they are frequently unprotected and a prime target for cybercriminals. When possible, avoid using public Wi-Fi for sensitive activities such as online banking and purchasing, and instead employ a VPN.

9. Regularly reviewing your bank and credit card statements will assist you in identifying any unauthorized expenditures or suspicious activity. Set up alerts for your accounts so that you are immediately notified of any suspicious activity.

10. Consider sharing sensitive information such as your full name, address, and phone number online with caution. This information

can be used by cybercriminals to hijack your identity and gain access to your accounts.

In the digital era, protecting your personal information online is essential. By adhering to these guidelines, you can decrease your likelihood of becoming a victim of cybercrime and protect your sensitive data. remain vigilant and remain safe!

Chapter 7: Cybersecurity for Small Businesses: Best Practices for Protecting Your Organization

• *An overview of the cyber-threats facing small enterprises*

Small businesses are a vital component of any economy, and in the modern era, technology has become indispensable to their operation. However, as reliance on technology increases, so does exposure to cybersecurity threats. Small businesses are especially susceptible to cyberattacks because they may lack the resources necessary to secure themselves adequately.

Small businesses encounter a variety of cyber-threats, and it is crucial to be aware of these dangers in order to protect against them. Phishing attacks are one of the most prevalent types of cyberattacks. Phishing attacks are intended to deceive victims into divulging sensitive information, such as passwords and credit card numbers. These assaults may arrive via email, text message, or social media messages.

Malware is a prevalent cybersecurity risk for small businesses. Malware is a form of malicious software that is designed to damage or exploit computer systems. Malware can be used to pilfer sensitive information, monitor online activity, and even remotely control computer systems. Through email attachments, software downloads, and malicious websites, malware can propagate.

Another significant threat to small enterprises is ransomware. Ransomware is a form of malicious software that encrypts the victim's files and renders them inaccessible until a ransom is paid. Small businesses can be devastated by ransomware attacks, which can result in the loss of vital data and the inability to operate routinely.

Small enterprises are also susceptible to website attacks. Code vulnerabilities can be exploited by hackers to obtain access to sensitive data or take control of a website. This can lead to data breaches or the introduction of malicious code onto the website.

Lastly, insider threats can also affect modest businesses. When an employee or contractor intentionally or unintentionally causes damage to the company's information systems, this is referred to as an insider threat. This may involve the seizure of sensitive data or the introduction of malicious code into the organization's systems.

Small enterprises must take proactive measures to secure their systems against these threats. This includes instituting strong passwords, updating software and systems on a regular basis, and providing employees with cybersecurity best practices training. Small businesses should also consider purchasing cybersecurity insurance to safeguard themselves from the financial consequences of a cyberattack.

In addition to these preventative measures, small businesses must also have an incident response plan in place. This plan should include measures to mitigate the damage, such as disconnecting infected systems from the network, and measures to rapidly restore normal operations.

Small businesses encounter a variety of cyberthreats, and it is crucial to be aware of these dangers in order to protect against them. Implementing robust cybersecurity practices, such as regular system updates and employee training, can aid in the prevention of cyberattacks. In the event of a cybersecurity incident, it is crucial to have a response plan in place to minimize the damage and restore normal operations as soon as feasible.

• *How to develop a business cybersecurity plan*

As businesses become more reliant on technology to conduct operations, cybersecurity has become a top priority. Due to their limited resources and the misconception that they are less likely to be targeted, small businesses are particularly vulnerable to cyber threats. However, small businesses are just as susceptible to cyberattacks as large corporations, making it imperative that they have a cybersecurity plan in place.

Creating a cybersecurity plan requires not only implementing the appropriate technology, but also fostering a cybersecurity culture within the organization. Employees play a crucial role in protecting a company's data and systems, so it is crucial to educate and train them on the significance of cybersecurity and how to identify and respond to cyber threats.

The following are measures that small businesses can take to develop a cybersecurity plan:

1. Conduct a Risk Assessment: A risk assessment assists in identifying potential data and system vulnerabilities and hazards. This procedure involves identifying the data and assets that require protection, evaluating the likelihood and impact of prospective threats, and assessing the organization's current security measures.

2. Develop a Cybersecurity Policy: A cybersecurity policy details the organization's protocols for protecting its data and systems. This policy should include password management, data backup, access control, and incident response guidelines.

3. Training employees is essential for establishing a culture of cybersecurity. Employees must be educated on the risks associated with cyber threats, how to identify and respond to fraudulent emails, how to secure their devices, and the organization's cybersecurity policies and procedures.

4. Implement Security Measures To protect their data and systems, small enterprises should implement security measures. Firewalls, anti-virus software, encryption, and multi-factor authentication may be among these measures.

5. Regularly Update and Test Security Measures Due to the constant evolution of cyber threats, it is essential to update and test

security measures on a regular basis to ensure their effectiveness. This process may involve evaluating the company's incident response plan, conducting vulnerability assessments, and patching software vulnerabilities.

6. Small businesses should have an incident response plan in place to respond swiftly and effectively to a cyberattack. This plan should include measures for containing and mitigating the attack, notifying affected parties, and restoring normal operations.

7. Small businesses should continually monitor and evaluate their cybersecurity plan to ensure that it remains effective. This procedure may involve evaluating security logs, analyzing security incidents, and revising policies and procedures as required.

Small businesses face a unique set of cybersecurity challenges, but with the proper plan in place, they can safeguard their data and systems against cyberattacks. By conducting a risk assessment, creating a cybersecurity policy, training employees, implementing security measures, regularly updating and testing those measures, having an incident response plan, and continuously monitoring and reviewing their plan, small businesses can create a cybersecurity culture that protects their organization.

• *Best practices for securing the data and network of your organization*

Cybersecurity is a vital concern for all businesses. Small enterprises are particularly susceptible to cyber threats due to their limited resources and knowledge. Therefore, it is essential to develop a cybersecurity strategy that prioritizes the protection of your company's data and network. Here are some recommended practices for securing the data and network of your business:

• Conduct a Risk Assessment: Prior to developing a cybersecurity plan, it is crucial to comprehend the potential threats and vulnerabilities. A risk assessment will assist you in identifying potential hazards, evaluating their likelihood and impact, and determining the most suitable countermeasures.

• Establish Security Policies: Create and implement comprehensive security policies that define expectations and guidelines for employee conduct, including data access, network usage, password creation and usage, and internet usage policies.

• Educate Employees: Employees are frequently the weakest component in the cybersecurity defense of an organization. Regular training and awareness sessions can assist employees in identifying and avoiding prevalent cyber threats such as phishing, social engineering, and malware attacks.

• Secure Your Network: Ensure the security of your network infrastructure by employing firewalls, intrusion detection systems, and other security software to manage and monitor network traffic.

• Update and Patch Your Software: Regularly update and patch your software and operating systems to prevent cybercriminals from exploiting known vulnerabilities.

• Backup Your Data: Regularly backup all vital data and store backups offsite. Regular backups safeguard your data against accidental or malicious deletion, hardware failure, natural disasters, and cyber-attacks.

Implement access controls to restrict who has access to data and systems and under what conditions. Passwords, multi-factor authentication, and role-based access controls comprise the access controls.

• Monitor Network Activity: Continually monitor your network activity for any anomalous behavior that could indicate a security breach. Logging all user activity, such as email and web browsing, can provide valuable insights into the health of your network and assist in identifying security incidents.

• Test Your Security Measures Regularly: Regularly testing your security measures will help you identify vulnerabilities and weaknesses in your security infrastructure before they can be exploited.

Even with the finest security measures in place, a security breach may still occur. Having an incident response plan in place will allow you to respond swiftly and efficiently in order to minimize damage, recover lost data, and prevent future incidents.

Data and network security requires a combination of technology, policies, and employee education. By implementing the aforementioned best practices, you can develop a comprehensive cybersecurity plan to safeguard your company's assets from cyber threats. Keep in mind that cyber threats are constantly evolving, so testing and updating your security measures on a regular basis is necessary to remain ahead of cybercriminals.

• *The significance of employee cybersecurity education and training*

As businesses become increasingly dependent on technology, their susceptibility to cyberattacks increases. Small businesses may be targeted by hackers for a variety of reasons, including gaining access to consumer data, stealing intellectual property, and holding data for ransom. Educating employees on cybersecurity best practices is one of the most effective methods to defend a company against cyberattacks.

Employees are frequently the weakest component in the cybersecurity defense of a company. This is due to the fact that they may be unaware of the risks associated with cyberattacks or how to recognize prospective threats. Employees may inadvertently open phishing emails, download malware, or utilize weak passwords. A single employee error can place the entire organization at risk.

To safeguard your business, you must establish a cybersecurity culture. This necessitates that all employees comprehend the significance of cybersecurity and adopt measures to safeguard company data. Education and training of employees is one of the most effective methods for fostering a cybersecurity culture.

Training employees on cybersecurity best practices can aid in preventing cyberattacks, lowering the risk of data breaches, and safeguarding sensitive company data. Here are some exemplary employee education and training practices:

1. Establish policies and procedures. A company's cybersecurity policy should outline employee expectations and provide guidelines for the secure use of technology. The policy should address password management, email usage, and the use of personal devices on company networks.

2. Cybersecurity training should be continuous in order to keep employees abreast of the latest threats and best practices. This may

consist of periodic seminars, online training courses, or simulated phishing attacks.

3. Employees should be encouraged to report suspicious activity, such as phishing emails or peculiar network activity. Reporting incidents can aid in preventing additional damage and provide valuable data for future prevention efforts.

4. Utilize real-world examples: Using real-world examples of cyberattacks can assist employees in comprehending the hazards and significance of cybersecurity. This may include successful examples of phishing emails, ransomware attacks, or data intrusions.

5. Cybersecurity training can be dull and uninteresting, but it doesn't have to be. Incorporate interactive elements into the training, such as quizzes, activities, and videos.

There are several other best practices for securing a company's data and network, in addition to employee education and training. These consist of:

1. Implementing firewalls and antivirus software can aid in preventing unauthorized access and detecting and removing malware.

2. Encourage employees to use strong passwords and implement a policy mandating regular password changes.

3. Limiting access to sensitive data: Not all employees require access to sensitive data. Limiting access can aid in decreasing the likelihood of data intrusions.

4. Regularly storing up data ensures that it will not be lost in the event of a cyberattack.

5. Updating software and operating systems on a regular basis: Software and operating systems should be updated on a regular basis to address any security vulnerabilities.

Education and instruction of employees are essential to a company's cybersecurity defense. Businesses can reduce the risk of cyberattacks and safeguard sensitive data by establishing a culture of cybersecurity and implementing best practices for securing data and networks.

Chapter 8: Cybersecurity for Children: Best Practices for Keeping Children Online Safe

• *Being aware of the specific dangers associated with minors and the Internet*

The internet is an extensive and intricate network that provides a variety of benefits, including educational resources, communication platforms, and entertainment. However, it poses a number of unique risks, especially to minors. As technology continues to advance, it is crucial that parents, educators, and other caregivers recognize these risks and take steps to safeguard children online.

Inappropriate content is one of the most significant risks associated with minors and the Internet. The Internet provides access to a broad variety of content, some of which may not be appropriate for young children. This can include explicit material, acts of violence, hate speech, and other detrimental content. In addition, children may accidentally discover inappropriate content while seeking for something else.

To mitigate this risk, it is essential to monitor children's Internet utilization and implement content-filtering software. Numerous internet service providers provide parental controls that can be activated to filter content and limit access to specific websites. Parents and caregivers should also discuss appropriate online behavior with children and establish clear internet usage boundaries.

Cyberbullying is another significant risk associated with minors and the Internet. Cyberbullying is a form of bullying that takes place online, and it can be just as damaging as traditional abuse. Cyberbullying can take many forms, including the dissemination of rumors, the distribution of embarrassing photographs or videos, and the transmission of threatening messages. This can be especially distressing for children, who may feel helpless in the face of the tormenting.

To protect children from cyberbullying, it is vital to educate them on appropriate online conduct and how to identify and report mistreatment. In addition to monitoring children's social media accounts, parents and caregivers should encourage them to speak up if they witness or experience cyberbullying. It is essential to take reports of cyberbullying seriously and implement the necessary measures to stop the behavior.

In addition to cyberbullying, online predators may also pose a threat to minors. Online predators are individuals who target minors for sexual exploitation or other forms of abuse via the

Internet. These predators may utilize social media, online games, or chat rooms to acquire children's trust and manipulate them into meeting in person.

To protect children from online predators, it is crucial to educate them on proper online conduct and the risks of interacting with strangers online. Parents and guardians should monitor their children's online behavior and report any suspicious behavior or communication to the proper authorities. Educating children about online privacy and the significance of not sharing personal information online is also crucial.

Children may also be vulnerable to identity theft and other forms of online financial deception. Personal information pertaining to children, such as their Social Security numbers, can be used to establish credit accounts and obtain loans. This may have an enduring effect on their financial security.

To protect children from online identity theft and financial fraud, it is crucial to monitor their online activity and educate them on the significance of keeping personal information private. In order to prevent identity theft, parents and guardians should also consider freezing their children's credit reports and frequently check for suspicious activity.

The Internet provides numerous advantages for children, but it also poses unique dangers. Parents, caregivers, and educators must take measures to safeguard children online, such as monitoring internet usage, filtering inappropriate content, conversing with children about online behavior, and reporting suspicious activity to the proper authorities. By comprehending these risks and proactively mitigating them, we can assist in keeping children safe online.

• *Suggestions for parental controls and surveillance*

It is essential for parents to be aware of the hazards associated with their children's online activity, given the growing use of the internet and technology by children. The internet can be a valuable learning and exploration tool for children, but it can also expose them to potential perils such as cyberbullying, online predators, and inappropriate content. Parents can employ parental controls and monitoring to safeguard their children online.

Parental controls are tools and configurations that restrict children's access to specific websites, applications, and content. These controls can be configured on mobile devices, tablets, and computers. Numerous operating systems and internet service providers include parental control options that can be tailored to the user's age and preferences.

Common parental controls include filtering and barring content, limiting device usage time, and restricting access to specific apps or features. For instance, parents can configure filters to block websites containing explicit material, violence, or hate speech. Additionally, they can limit the amount of time children spend on their devices and restrict access to social media and messaging applications during specific hours.

Monitoring can be an effective addition to parental controls for keeping children secure online. Monitoring is the practice of observing children's online activities, including their browsing history, search queries, and social media interactions. This can aid parents in identifying potential dangers and addressing them before they become an issue.

Parents have access to numerous monitoring tools, including applications and software that can be installed on mobile devices. These tools enable parents to monitor their children's online activity in real-time and receive alerts if they encounter potential dangers. Some tools also provide geolocation tracking, which enables parents to know their children's geographic location at all times.

When implementing parental controls and monitoring, it is essential for parents and children to communicate candidly. Children must be made aware of the rules and restrictions in place and comprehend why they are necessary. Parents can use these resources to teach their children about online safety and responsible Internet use.

Parental controls and surveillance should not serve as a replacement for parental supervision and guidance. These instruments can be useful in reducing children's exposure to potential dangers, but they are not foolproof. Parents should continue to be engaged in their children's online activities and have candid discussions with them about their online experiences.

In addition to parental controls and supervision, parents can take additional measures to safeguard their children online. For instance, they can instruct their children on secure online conduct, such as not sharing personal information or meeting strangers in person. They can also encourage their children to approach them if they encounter issues or have queries regarding their online activity.

Parental controls and monitoring can be effective safeguards for children's online safety. Parents can protect their children from potential dangers such as cyberbullying and online predators by implementing these controls and monitoring their children's activity. However, parents must maintain open communication with their children, educate them about online safety, and remain involved in their online activities.

• Best practices for cybersecurity education for minors

The Internet has become an integral part of our existence, and as a result, it has become an indispensable resource for the education, entertainment, and social interaction of children. However, as with any tool, there are risks associated with the Internet, and it is essential that children be taught how to remain secure online. This article will discuss the most effective methods for educating youth about cybersecurity.

It is never too early to begin educating children about online security. Even young infants can comprehend fundamental concepts such as not speaking to strangers, and the same holds true for the internet. Start by teaching them not to share personal information online, including their name, address, and phone number. Also, inform them that they should only communicate with individuals they know and trust.

Children must feel secure talking to their parents or guardians about their online experiences, including any potentially dangerous or uncomfortable situations. Encourage open dialogue by letting them know they can approach you with any inquiries or concerns regarding their online activities.

It is essential to use age-appropriate language and explanations when teaching children about cybersecurity. Children of a younger age may not comprehend sophisticated technical terms, but they can comprehend concepts such as avoiding strangers and sharing personal information. As they age, you can introduce them to more complex concepts such as online privacy, social media security, and password protection.

Children need to realize that anything they post online can have long-lasting repercussions. Explain that anything they post online can be viewed by anyone, including prospective employers, college admissions officers, and even future romantic companions. Encourage them to consider how their online activities may affect their future before posting and to deliberate carefully before they do so.

Passwords are one of the most important aspects of online security. Teach children the significance of using strong, unique passwords for each of their accounts and never sharing them. Consider using a password manager to secure their password management.

Teach them how to recognize phishing attempts. Phishing is a form of online fraud in which cybercriminals attempt to fool individuals into divulging sensitive information such as passwords, credit card numbers, and social security numbers. Teach children to identify and avoid fraud attempts by keeping an eye out for suspicious emails, text messages, and phone calls. Encourage them to confirm the authenticity of any requests for personal information with a responsible adult.

Social media is a popular method for children to connect with friends and share their lives, but it can also lead to cyberbullying and other online dangers. Establish explicit guidelines for the use of social media, including what types of content can be posted, who can be connected with, and how to report cyberbullying or inappropriate behavior.

Children learn by example, so it is imperative that you demonstrate appropriate online conduct. Avoid oversharing personal information online, use secure passwords, and exercise caution when posting on social media. By demonstrating appropriate online conduct, you can assist your children in developing healthful online habits.

In today's digital era, it is vital to educate children about cybersecurity. By instructing them on online safety, privacy, and security, you can assist them in developing lifelong, beneficial online habits. To help your children remain safe online, remember to be approachable, use age-appropriate language, and model good online behavior.

• *Safeguarding your child's personal data online*

As children increasingly use the internet for socializing, education, and entertainment, it is crucial for parents to safeguard their personal information online. Children may not comprehend the risks associated with sharing personal information, making them especially susceptible to identity theft and other online dangers. Here are some suggestions for safeguarding your child's online privacy:

1. Teach your infant to maintain confidentiality of personal data

Children should comprehend that personal information, such as their full name, address, phone number, and date of birth, should never be disclosed online without the consent of a parent or other responsible adult. This includes social media platforms, gaming platforms, and online forums. Encourage your child to consider twice before sharing personal information online, and to always consult with you first.

2. Use security measures

Numerous websites and apps have privacy settings that enable you to regulate who can view your child's personal information and what content they can access. Review and alter these settings on all websites and applications your child uses. You can also enable privacy settings on your child's device, such as blocking access to specific apps and websites.

3. Monitor your child's Internet usage.

Monitor your child's online behavior, including their use of social media, online entertainment, and web browsing. This will enable you to identify any potential risks or threats and protect your child's personal data. You can use parental controls to restrict your child's access to specific websites and applications, as well as to monitor their online activity.

4. Use strong credentials

Ensure that your child uses secure passwords for all of their accounts, including social media, email, and gaming. Encourage them to use a password that combines letters, numerals, and special characters, and to avoid using the same password for multiple accounts. You can also use a password manager to help your child remember and secure their passwords.

5. Discuss with your infant online safety

Talking to your child about online safety is the most essential thing you can do to protect their personal information online. Explain the risks associated with sharing personal information online and instruct them on how to recognize and avoid online threats like phishing, malware, and identity theft. Encourage them to approach you if they ever feel unsafe or uneasy online.

Children can be educated about the significance of protecting their personal information online through the use of entertaining examples. For instance, you and your child can play a game in which you and your child take turns sharing personal information, such as your full name, address, and phone number, and then determine which information is real and which is fake. This can help teach your child that personal information is valuable and should be kept private.

Create a "secret agent" game in which your child must secure their personal data from "online spies" This may entail setting up strong passwords, utilizing privacy settings on social media accounts, and recognizing phishing scams.

By safeguarding your child's personal information online, you can protect them from identity theft and other online threats. It is crucial to remember that children may not comprehend the risks associated with sharing personal information online; therefore, it is the responsibility of parents to take preventative measures to safeguard their children.

Chapter 9: The Future of Cybersecurity: Emerging Trends and Best Practices

• *Discussion of emerging cyber-threats and trends*

The field of cybersecurity is ever-changing, with new threats and trends surfacing frequently. To effectively safeguard ourselves and our digital assets, it is essential to remain informed of these alterations. This article will provide an overview of some of the most recent emerging threats and trends in cybersecurity.

Ransomware is one of the most prominent emerging cybersecurity hazards. Ransomware is a form of malware that encrypts the files of a victim and demands payment in exchange for the decryption key. In recent years, ransomware attacks have increased in frequency and sophistication. Some ransomware assaults, in addition to encrypting files, steal sensitive data and threaten to release it unless the victim pays the ransom.

Hackers' use of artificial intelligence (AI) and machine learning (ML) is a growing hazard to cybersecurity. AI and ML can be utilized to create more effective and efficient attacks and to evade detection more effectively. Using AI and ML, for instance, hackers could analyze a target's behavior and generate more convincing fraudulent emails.

Internet of Things (IoT) devices are also gaining popularity as cyberattack targets. Numerous IoT devices have inadequate security measures, making them susceptible to hijacking. Using compromised IoT devices, hackers can launch attacks against other targets or pilfer sensitive data.

Phishing attacks are a well-known cybersecurity threat, but they continue to evolve and become increasingly sophisticated. Spear phishing is a form of targeted espionage that is tailored to a particular individual or organization. In order to construct a convincing phishing email, hackers may use publicly available information about the target, such as their job title and employer.

The use of zero-day vulnerabilities by hackers is a second trend in cybersecurity. Zero-day vulnerabilities are software vulnerabilities that have not yet been patched and are undisclosed to the software vendor. Zero-day vulnerabilities allow hackers to launch attacks that are challenging to detect and defend against.

In addition to these emerging hazards, there are some new cybersecurity trends that merit consideration. The shift toward cloud-based security solutions is one of these. The advantages of cloud-based security over traditional on-premises security solutions include simpler administration and scalability.

The use of automation and orchestration is another trend in cybersecurity. Automation and orchestration can help to expedite security processes and reduce response times to incidents. For instance, automated threat detection and response can expedite the identification and neutralization of threats.

The use of artificial intelligence and machine learning is increasing in the field of cybersecurity. AI and ML can be used to analyze massive data sets and identify patterns that may indicate a security threat. Anomalies in user behavior, which may indicate a compromised account, can also be identified using these tools.

To remain protected against these emerging threats and trends, it is essential to adopt cybersecurity best practices. These include maintaining up-to-date software and operating systems, employing robust passwords and multi-factor authentication, and utilizing antivirus software and firewalls. Additionally, it is essential to regularly backup and test backups to ensure that they are functioning effectively.

It is also essential to educate employees and family members on cybersecurity best practices. This includes teaching them to recognize fraudulent emails and suspicious websites and encouraging them to report any suspicious behavior.

Constantly evolving cybersecurity threats and trends necessitate that we remain informed in order to effectively secure ourselves and our digital assets. By employing cybersecurity best practices and remaining current on the most recent threats and trends, we can ensure that our data and devices remain secure.

• *Best practices for keeping abreast of evolving cyber-threats*

As technology progresses, so do cyber-threats. Keeping up with new hazards and trends is essential for maintaining security. Here are some recommended practices for keeping abreast of cyber-threats:

1. Stay Informed: Subscribe to cybersecurity journals and newsletters to stay abreast of the most recent cybersecurity threats and trends. There are numerous credible sources that offer current information on the most recent hazards and vulnerabilities. The cyber security journals KrebsOnSecurity, Dark Reading, and ThreatPost are quite popular.

2. Attend Conferences and Events: Attend cybersecurity conferences and events to keep abreast of the newest developments and to network with other cybersecurity professionals. RSA Conference, Black Hat, and DEF CON are three well-known cybersecurity conferences.

3. Participate in Cybersecurity Communities: Join cybersecurity communities and forums to interact with other cybersecurity professionals and to discuss the most recent threats and vulnerabilities. Popular cybersecurity communities include r/netsec on Reddit, the Cybersecurity community on Hashnode, and The Hacker News community.

4. Conduct Regular Security Assessments: Conduct regular security assessments to identify vulnerabilities and deficiencies in the security posture of your organization. This will allow you to anticipate emerging hazards and trends.

5. Maintaining Software and Systems: Maintain software and systems with the most recent upgrades and updates. This will ensure that you have the most recent security patches for all identified vulnerabilities.

6. Conduct Regular Employee Training: Conduct regular employee training on cybersecurity best practices to ensure that your staff is aware of the most recent threats and trends. This will prevent them from falling victim to social engineering and other cyber hazards.

7. Implement Multifactor Authentication: Multifactor authentication (MFA) should be implemented on all systems and applications. MFA is an additional security measure that necessitates the use of multiple authentication methods, such as a password and a biometric factor, before granting access.

8. Utilize Advanced Threat Detection Tools: Identify and respond to threats in real-time using advanced threat detection tools. These tools use machine learning and other sophisticated techniques to identify threats that signature-based tools may overlook.

9. Implement a Cyber Incident Response Plan To ensure that your organization is prepared to respond to a cyber-attack, implement a cyber incident response plan. This plan should include procedures for identifying and containing an attack, notifying relevant parties, and restoring systems and data.

10. Collaborate with Trusted Cybersecurity Partners: Collaborate with trusted cybersecurity partners to remain abreast of emerging threats and trends. These partners can provide you with the most

up-to-date threat intelligence, security evaluations, and incident response services to keep you safe.

Keeping abreast of emerging cybersecurity threats and trends is crucial for maintaining security in the digital age. By adhering to these best practices, you can help ensure that your organization is equipped to detect and respond to the most recent cyber threats.

• Anticipating the future of cybersecurity

As technology continues to advance and more of our lives migrate online, it is impossible to overstate the significance of cybersecurity. It is imperative to be prepared for the future of cybersecurity as cyber threats are constantly evolving.

Here are some cybersecurity best practices for preparing for the future.

• Remain Current on Emerging Threats and Trends: As technology progresses, new threats and trends will emerge in the cybersecurity landscape. It is crucial to remain current on emerging hazards and trends in order to be able to defend against them. Regularly reading industry publications, attending conferences and seminars, and keeping up with the latest cybersecurity news can help you remain ahead of the competition.

Adopt a proactive approach to cybersecurity, rather than waiting for a cyber-attack to occur and then reacting. This entails routinely evaluating your security policies and procedures, identifying potential vulnerabilities, and addressing them before they are exploited. Regular security assessments and penetration testing can assist you in identifying vulnerabilities and validating that your security controls are functioning as intended.

• Implement Advanced Security Technologies It is essential to implement advanced security technologies to protect against increasingly sophisticated cyber threats. This includes technologies such as artificial intelligence and machine learning, which can assist in identifying and responding to hazards in real time. Implementing technologies such as multifactor authentication and encryption can also improve your security posture.

• Train Employees on Cybersecurity Best Practices Employees can be a weak link in the cybersecurity defenses of your organization. It is essential to educate employees on cybersecurity best practices, such as how to recognize and avoid phishing scams, how to establish strong passwords, and how to identify and report suspicious activity. Regular security awareness training can ensure that your employees are aware of the most recent hazards and best practices.

• Create an Incident Response Plan: No matter how well-prepared you are, a cyber-attack is always a possibility. Creating an incident response plan can help ensure that your organization is prepared to respond swiftly and effectively in the event of an attack. This plan should include procedures for identifying and containing the assault, as well as procedures for notifying stakeholders and recovering from the attack.

• Collaborate with a Reliable Security Provider: As the sophistication of cyber threats increases, it can be difficult to keep up with the most recent technologies and best practices. Partnering with a reputable security provider can aid in protecting your organization from emerging hazards. A security provider can offer expert advice on cybersecurity best practices, as well as access to cutting-edge security technologies and threat intelligence.

As technology advances and cyber threats become more sophisticated, cybersecurity will continue to evolve in the future. By staying current on emerging threats and trends, adopting a proactive approach to cybersecurity, implementing advanced security technologies, training employees on best practices, developing an incident response plan, and partnering with a reputable security provider, you can help ensure that your organization is well-equipped to defend against cyber threats in the present and future.

Chapter 10: Tenth Chapter: Concluding Remarks and a Call to Action

• *Recap of the book's essential takeaways*

Individuals must be vigilant against social engineering techniques designed to manipulate and deceive them into divulging personal information or clicking on malicious links, in addition to employing best practices for device security and safe browsing habits. Personal and business information must also be safeguarded using best practices for secure communication and identity protection online.

Additionally, small businesses must be aware of the cybersecurity threats they confront and take measures to protect their data and networks. This includes the creation of a cybersecurity plan, the implementation of best practices for securing company data and networks, and the provision of cybersecurity education and training to employees.

Parents must also implement parental controls and monitor their children's online activities, educate their children on cybersecurity best practices, and safeguard their children's online personal information.

New cybersecurity hazards and trends will continue to emerge as technology continues to advance. To guarantee personal and business security, it is essential to remain current on these emerging hazards and to implement best practices.

Cybersecurity is an important issue in the digital world of today, with the potential to affect individuals, corporations, and governments. Individuals and businesses can protect themselves from cyber threats by employing best practices for device security, safe browsing habits, social engineering avoidance, secure communication, online identity protection, and employee education and training. In addition, individuals and organizations can be proactive in preparing for the future of cybersecurity by remaining current on emerging trends and threats.

• *Call to action for implementing best practices in cybersecurity*

In the digital age, cybersecurity threats are becoming more prevalent and sophisticated. It is essential to be aware of the risks and hazards and to take the necessary precautions to safeguard oneself, one's family, one's business, and one's online identity. This book has covered a variety of topics, such as establishing a solid security foundation, safe browsing practices, social engineering, secure communication, managing your online identity, and cybersecurity for small businesses and children.

To implement these best practices, we encourage readers to adopt them into their daily lives. Here are some actions you can perform immediately:

Regularly update your devices, software, and operating systems.

Use unique, robust passwords for all of your online accounts, and consider using a password manager.

Educate yourself and your family on best practices for cybersecurity, such as secure browsing habits and social engineering techniques.

Invest in reputable antivirus software and run regular scans on your devices.

Employ secure communication tools, such as end-to-end encrypted messaging applications, and avoid disclosing personal information over public Wi-Fi networks.

Monitor your online presence and implement security measures for your social media accounts.

Develop a cybersecurity plan for your small business and educate your employees on best practices for protecting the data and network of your company.

Instruct your children on appropriate online conduct and use parental controls to restrict their access to specific websites and applications.

You can safeguard yourself and your loved ones from cyber threats by implementing these best practices. We urge you to take action now and remain vigilant against future cyber threats.

• Perspectives on the future of cybersecurity and the significance of continuing education and awareness.

Cybersecurity is an ever-evolving discipline, with new risks and threats constantly emerging. As our daily reliance on technology increases, the significance of cybersecurity will only continue to grow. In this article, we will examine the outlook for cybersecurity in the future, as well as the necessity of ongoing education and awareness in safeguarding ourselves and our digital assets.

Cybercrime's expanding threat is one of the most significant developments in cybersecurity. The Internet Crime Complaint Center (IC3) of the FBI reports that cybercrime reports increased by 69.4% between 2019 and 2020. These attacks can take many forms, including phishing and ransomware, and they can have devastating effects on individuals, enterprises, and governments.

Cybersecurity professionals must also contend with the emergence of new technologies, such as the Internet of Things (IoT) and artificial intelligence (AI), in addition to the expanding threat of cybercrime. These technologies offer enormous potential advantages, but also introduce new security hazards. IoT devices, for instance, are notoriously insecure, making them an attractive target for hackers seeking network access. Meanwhile, cyberattacks powered by artificial intelligence could be significantly more sophisticated and difficult to detect than traditional attacks, making them even more hazardous.

To remain abreast of these threats, cybersecurity experts must continuously adapt and update their skills and knowledge. Consequently, ongoing education and awareness are essential elements of any cybersecurity strategy. Cybersecurity professionals must remain current on the most recent threats and trends, and they must be able to respond swiftly and effectively to an attack.

Attending industry conferences and events is one of the best ways to remain up-to-date on the most recent threats and trends in cybersecurity. These events offer the chance to network with other professionals in the field, acquire knowledge of new technologies and techniques, and gain insight into emerging threats. Numerous conferences also provide training sessions and workshops, allowing attendees to receive practical experience with the most recent tools and technologies.

Employee training is an essential element of ongoing cybersecurity education and awareness. Too often, cybersecurity vulnerabilities are caused by human error, such as clicking on a phishing link or using a password that is too weak. By regularly training employees on cybersecurity best practices, businesses can substantially reduce their risk of falling victim to a cyberattack. This training should include topics such as password management, secure browsing practices, and the ability to recognize and avoid phishing scams.

As the threat environment continues to evolve, it becomes increasingly essential for individuals to assume responsibility for their own cybersecurity. This includes using strong passwords, keeping software up-to-date, and avoiding suspicious emails and websites. It also entails keeping abreast of the most recent hazards and taking precautions to safeguard yourself and your digital assets.

Fortunately, there are a variety of resources available to assist individuals and organizations in staying informed about cybersecurity best practices. The National Institute of Standards and Technology (NIST), for instance, has published a Cybersecurity Framework that provides a comprehensive set of guidelines for defending against cyber threats. The framework covers topics including risk assessment, threat detection, and incident response, and is an excellent resource for businesses seeking to enhance their cybersecurity posture.

In addition to the NIST framework, there are numerous online training programs for cybersecurity. These programs can range from free webinars and online courses to paid training programs that provide in-depth training and certification for a fee. These resources can be an excellent method for individuals seeking to improve their cybersecurity skills to remain current on the most recent threats and trends.

The outlook for cybersecurity in the future is one of constant change and development. As technology progresses, new hazards and dangers will continue to emerge. The only way to remain ahead of these threats is to maintain a commitment to ongoing education and vigilance. As our personal and professional lives become increasingly dependent on technology, cybersecurity threats will continue to evolve and become more sophisticated. To remain ahead of these threats and protect sensitive information and systems, individuals and organizations must prioritize cybersecurity education, awareness, and investment. Through collaboration and vigilance, we can assure a safer and more secure digital future.